AMONG ANCIENT

AMONG ANCIENT RUINS

THE LEGACY of EARL H. MORRIS

UNIVERSITY OF COLORADO MUSEUM
INTRODUCTION BY JOE BEN WHEAT

Edited by Frederick W. Lange and Diana Leonard

JOHNSON BOOKS: BOULDER

Cover and text design: Christina Watkins
Frontispiece: Reconstructed polychrome pottery vessel from Kawaika-a

ISBN 0-933472-94-3
LCCCN 85-80408

Printed in the United States of America by
Johnson Publishing Company
1880 South 57th Court
Boulder, Colorado 80301

CONTENTS

Today the construction of a new museum is being begun at the university here, hence sometime during the coming year I shall have the job of installing the archaeological exhibits in it. It certainly will be a relief to see the material that I have gathered at last in a fireproof structure.
—Earl Morris, letter to Emil Haury, 1937

FOREWORD

I absorbed Ann Axtell Morris's *Digging in the Southwest* during one of many teenage summers spent working on Pueblo site excavations in the Rio Grande Valley. The summer of my sophomore year in high school I participated in the salvage of a Basket Maker II pithouse complex near Tohatchi in northwestern New Mexico; thereafter I worked mostly in Central America and Mesoamerica. When I came to the University of Colorado in 1983, photographs from the University Museum's very successful exhibit "Among Ancient Ruins: The Explorations of Earl H. Morris," developed with the aid of a grant from the Colorado Humanities Council, were hanging in the second floor hallway. Needless to say, the vistas brought back many memories.

As we planned the touring phase of the Morris exhibition, the idea of a small publication gradually developed. Not all of the photographs in this book are in the exhibition and vice versa; this is not a catalogue of the exhibition but a publication derived from it. Specifically, "Among Ancient Ruins" dealt only with Morris's Southwestern work, but here we have included brief coverage of his Mayan research. Also, the museum displays held a large quantity of artifacts recovered by Morris and now in the University of Colorado Museum collections; here we have included a few photographs of those artifacts.

Through the continuing use of his collections for comparative and innovative research, Earl H. Morris continues to be a presence in Southwestern archaeology. His importance is reflected in the exhibition and in this book. Morris was referring specifically to his work at Quirigua, Guatemala, when he wrote the following, but it might well stand as an assessment of his entire career: "I was privileged to rescue from oblivion and to help conserve for the enlightenment of future generations, certain creative efforts of unnamed aboriginal artists who were Masters in their times."

February 1985   Frederick W. Lange
                                                       Acting Curator, Anthropology
                                                       University of Colorado Museum

Earl Morris in the 1920s.

My heart is in the Southwestern field, and I know the Southwest portion of it if I know anything.
—Earl Morris, letter to Clark Wissler, 1922

PREFACE

Earl H. Morris was a world-renowned archaeologist, whose life and career of nearly 50 years roughly paralleled the growth and development of prehistoric research in the Southwest and Mesoamerica. He worked in the era of exploration during which many of the archaeological wonders of the world were first seen. The times also saw the advent of the automobile and other modern mechanical wonders. We forget the rigors and hardships endured by the early researchers. Horses were often the preferred means of transportation, and access to water and provisions were major concerns. Institutional funding for archaeological investigations was limited, and researchers such as Morris were frequently dependent for support on the interest and generosity of private individuals. Despite the difficulties, Morris's enthusiasm for archaeology stayed with him throughout his life and affected those who came in touch with him. As Hugo Rodeck, director emeritus of the University of Colorado Museum, recounted at the time of Morris's death:

> *He was a true gentleman, full of kindness and consideration. I never heard him utter an unkind word, nor say anything about anyone which was other than complimentary. It appears that his only means of speaking ill was to be unable to say much good. I do not know anyone who thought ill of him.*
>
> *Another of Earl's traits was his generosity. He was always willing to help in any way, and many a young scientist was privileged to share his vast fund of archaeological knowledge and humane wisdom. His kindly willingness to serve others, even at the cost of his own interests, has been an invariable feature of his relations with the Museum and its personnel.*

When Morris wrote or spoke about archaeology, it was in polished, well-turned phrases. Writing was difficult for Morris, as it is for most of us; inevitably the lure of

SAN JUAN DRAINAGE CHRONOLOGIES

YEARS, A.D.	Morris' Chronology 1920-27	Pecos Classification 1927	Roberts' Classification 1935
1300	Full Pueblo (open sites)	Pueblo III	Great Pueblo
1200	Cliff Dweller (cave sites)		
1100			
1000	Late Pre Pueblo	Pueblo II	Developmental Pueblo
900	Early Pre Pueblo or Slab House		
800		Pueblo I	
700			
600	Post Basket Maker	Basket Maker III	Modified Basket Maker
500			
400			
300	Basket Makers	Basket Maker II	Basket Maker
200			
100		- - - - - - - -	
0		Basket Maker I	- - - - - - - -

SELECTED ANASAZI PHASE SEQUENCES

	Mesa Verde Hayes (1964)	Chaco Canyon Hayes et. al. (1981)	Red Rock-Puerco Wendorf et. al. (1956)
YOUNGER	Mesa Verde	Late Pueblo III	Pueblo III
		Early Pueblo III	Wingate
	McElmo	Late Pueblo II	
			Late Pueblo II
	Mancos	Early Pueblo II	
	Ackmen		Red Mesa
	Piedra	Pueblo I	Kiatuthlanna
	Lino	Basketmaker III	White Mound
		Basketmaker II	
OLDER	Archaic	Archaic	

Earlier and more recent Southwestern chronology.

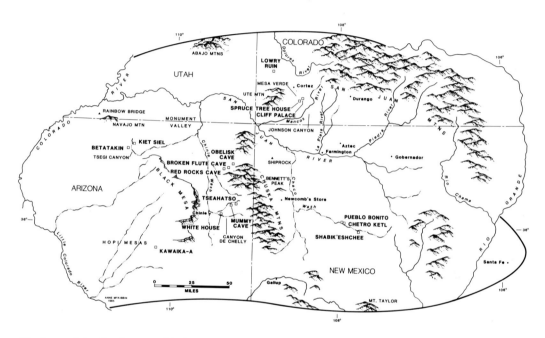

The heart of the Southwest, with the principal sites worked on by Earl H. Morris.

the trowel and shovel is stronger than the sense of duty to write. And he felt the weight and responsibility of his words. Nevertheless, Morris left a monumental legacy of published reports. He also left a large amount of unpublished work, some of which has been subsequently written up, but much remains to be studied and reported.

Morris is perhaps known best for his work in the Southwest, but he also made significant contributions to Mesoamerican archaeology. Likewise, he is mainly remembered for his excavations, but he was also responsible for site restorations at Aztec and Mesa Verde in the Southwest and at Chichen Itza in the Maya area.

THE EARLY YEARS

Earl Morris was born in Chama, New Mexico, on October 24, 1889, to Scott N. and Juliette Amanda (Halstead) Morris. His boyhood was spent in mining, sawmill, and construction camps. He traced his interest in archaeology to his earliest childhood, when ancient Indian artifacts were his first toys. These were found around camps in the San Juan region where his parents moved each winter to provide grass for their string of horses. "There was an artificial mound in the door yard of the adobe house where we lived that winter," Morris recalled, "and from it father exhumed a large collection of relics. The brightly painted bits of pottery that he tossed aside became my favorite playthings." Again, at Farmington, New Mexico, Morris noted:

> There was a ruin close to the log cabin we lived in. One morning
> in March of 1893, Father handed me a worn-out pick, the handle
> of which he had shortened to my length, and said, "Go dig in
> that hole where I worked yesterday, and you will be out of my
> way."

In this way, much as other parents might give a child an old baseball glove or some other tools for imitative behavior, Scott Morris introduced his son to his own enthusiasm for digging Indian relics. It was from these early experiences that Earl Morris's lifelong interest in the Basket Maker and Pueblo peoples of the Southwest developed.

Ironically, in light of Morris's later professional contributions, the kind of indiscriminate digging he was introduced to as a child destroys irreplaceable archaeological resources. On public and Indian reservation lands such activity is now illegal, but it was typical of the times Morris grew up in. Morris, the esteemed scientist, looked back at himself at age three and a half when there happened " . . . the clinching event that was to make of me an ardent pot hunter, who later on was to acquire the more creditable and I hope earned, classification as an archaeologist."

About his early education, Morris recalled, "My mother had been a teacher for many years and her experience both as a disciplinarian and an instructor enabled her to see to it that her only chick should not be found wanting in the three R's and a number of things besides."

His father was shot and killed during a disagreement with a business associate in December 1904 and, according to Florence and Robert Lister in their 1968 biography, this left young Earl ". . . bitter and introspective for the rest of his life," with his archaeological endeavors and the heavy physical labor his escape and emotional outlet.

BECOMING AN ARCHAEOLOGIST

Morris was fortunate enough to spend the summer of 1911 with Dr. Edgar L. Hewett in what is now Bandelier National Monument, New Mexico. In 1912 he went to Mesoamerica for the first time, again with Hewett, and spent the season at the Maya site of Quirigua in Guatemala. Morris recorded that:

> Seventy-five acres of land had been set aside by the United Fruit Company as a setting for the archaeological remains. Clearing of the center of the area left a strip of jungle, impenetrable to the eye, as periphery of the rectangle within which the principal ruins lay. Now and then a monkey peered down apprehensively from some tree-top. Pairs of gaudy macaws streaked the sky high overhead, and toward dusk smaller parrots by the thousand sought shelter for the night amidst the foliage of the jungle strip. . . . Due to the far-reaching vision of Samuel Zemurray, president of the United Fruit Company, the ruins there are and presumably will, in perpetuity be maintained as an archaeological park.

In 1913 Morris excavated cliff dweller sites in southwestern Colorado for the University of Colorado, and in the first months of 1914 he was back in Guatemala as Administrative Head of the fourth (and final) School of American Archaeology expedition to Quirigua. A falling out with Hewett, apparently over failed finances, ended Morris's involvement in the Maya area for the time.

Morris eventually received an A.B. degree from the University of Colorado in 1914 and an M.A. from the same institution the following year. During 1916-1917 he pursued advanced studies at Columbia but did not continue for the doctorate. After receiving his M.A. he was selected to work in the Rio Grande Valley with Nels C. Nelson, an archaeologist from the American Museum of Natural History in New York, who had been pioneering the technique of stratigraphic excavation in the Southwest. This early introduction to stratigraphy, along with a subsequent interest in tree-ring dating, provided the young Earl Morris with the opportunity to learn excavation and analytical techniques.

With these methods, archaeologists could for the first time demonstrate time depth and organize archaeological remains of Southwestern culture into approximate evolutionary sequences. Stratigraphic analysis had long been used in European geology and prehistory, but its application in the New World was just beginning. It would become a cornerstone of Southwestern archaeology. Stratigraphy can be explained by reference to a layer cake; the oldest layer is on the bottom (because it has to be put down first) and succeeding layers are each younger than the one before. Morris described "stratigraphic accumulations" as being similar to ". . . a book turned title page downward which one thence reads upwards."

Tree-ring dating, or dendrochronology, is based on the fact that certain trees grow thick rings in moist years and thin rings in dry years. Master charts were laboriously compiled at the University of Arizona using samples of wood from ruins from all over the Southwest (Morris himself providing the first samples). Once this was done, wood from a given prehistoric site could be analyzed by comparing its ring growth patterns into those on the master chart, thus obtaining an accurate date for when the wood was cut.

MORRIS
AND
HIS FAMILY

Elizabeth Ann, Earl, Lucille, and Sarah Lane Morris in front of their Boulder home, 1953.

It is difficult to realize that both girls are now fairly launched into a world of their own where sink or swim depends upon themselves rather than upon any guidance a parent can give.
—Earl Morris, letter to A. V. Kidder, 1950

Morris married twice. His first wife was Ann McCheane Axtell, also an archaeologist, whom he married in 1923 and who died in 1945 after a long illness. In 1923 Morris described her as ". . . my companion on all subsequent expeditions (after 1923), herself an archaeologist and an able collaborator in my work." His two daughters, Elizabeth Ann and Sarah Lane, were both by this first marriage. In the year following Ann Morris's death, Morris married Lucille Bowman, a popular teacher and principal at Highland School in Boulder.

11

Earl Morris at Bennett's Peak.

Pick and shovel are the tools of a lowly and misunderstood profession. There are almost as many different kinds of picks and shovels as there are artists' brushes, and each one is shaped for a definite and specific use to which it may be put with plundering stupidity or consummate skill. —Earl Morris, 1931

MORRIS, THE ARCHAEOLOGIST

The transition from Morris's early development to his establishment as an archaeologist began around 1915. He was almost unique among archaeologists working in the Southwest during this time as he was "home grown" and lived there year-round. Almost everyone else worked on the East Coast and commuted for the summers.

THE GOBERNADOR AREA

Beginning in 1915 Morris explored Gobernador Canyon and a series of related canyons in northern New Mexico. His survey located Pueblo I, Pueblo III, and historic period Pueblo sites, varying from caches of single artifacts to entire masonry pueblos. In addition to prehistoric materials of stone, bone, shell, and pottery, Morris and his two assistants found more recently manufactured items of Spanish origin—iron, copper, glass, and porcelain, a result of the Pueblo Indians taking refuge there with the Navajo after the revolt against the Spanish (1680-1692). That Navajo Indians as well as Jemez, Cochiti, and Tewa Pueblo Indians lived in the area is one of the most significant results from this research.

AZTEC RUIN

From 1917 to 1924 Morris worked as an archaeologist for the American Museum of Natural History, under whose sponsorship he explored the Aztec ruin in New Mexico and reconstructed the Great Kiva, some 48 feet in diameter. The Kiva was the first of its kind to be excavated and became a particular source of pride for Morris. "To excavate the Aztec Ruin," he wrote, "is a dream which had endured from my boyhood. . . ." The name "Aztec," incidentally, is a misnomer and did not originate with Morris. This and other terms, such as "Montezuma's Castle," reflect the early misconceptions of Southwesterners and others who presumed Mexican influence in the area. In reality these sites were constructed by Pueblo Indians.

Aztec Ruin was first mentioned in the Spanish accounts of the Dominguez-Escalante expedition of 1776-1777. Tree-ring dates indicate that the main construction period was between 1106 and 1121 A.D. Sandstone for building was transported from quarries two to four miles away, and roof timbers were obtained from mountains some 20 miles distant. The site represents the planned development of a major regional center, linked to small outlying communities.

Beginning in 1916 and continuing for over a decade, Morris directed the excavations of the Pueblo village at Aztec. He built a home there which has since become the visitors' center for the 27-acre Aztec National Monument.

BASKET MAKER

From 1925 until 1932, Earl Morris spent a number of field seasons in Canyon del Muerto, Arizona, and at numerous other sites on the Navajo Reservation. It was here that he sought evidence for the Basket Maker people inhabiting the canyons of the Southwest more than a thousand years earlier. In shallow caves along the sandstone cliffs Morris excavated sites from Basket Maker II through Pueblo III times. His work in the area is a landmark study of the diversity of Basket Maker industry and the richness of their arts.

Large quantities of beautifully preserved sandals were recovered during this research. Morris observed that "these people put into their sandals some of the most intricate hand weaving that has ever been done. They are known as the Basket Makers, but their work with sandals is even more ingenious." Morris collected over 1,000 finger-woven sandals, ranging in age from 700 to more than 1,700 years old. He noted that ". . . no two of the sandals are alike and there is endless variation in members of a pair. All of them are made by finger weaving without a loom to hamper the workers' artistic imagination." Morris thought that the men were the weavers and that such weaving was a specialized activity.

CHICHEN ITZA

After 1924 Morris was with the Carnegie Institution of Washington, D.C. At the invitation of Sylvanus G. Morley (with whom Morris had worked in Guatemala in 1912), he worked for five years directing the excavations and the reconstruction at the Temple of the Warriors at the Maya site of Chichen Itza on the Yucatan Peninsula. During the summers, when he was unable to work in the tropics, he continued work in Arizona, Colorado, New Mexico, and Utah; in 1926 he excavated at numerous sites in the Mimbres Valley of New Mexico. He was also at one time assistant curator of archaeology in the Natural History Museum in New York City.

NEW MEXICO AND ARIZONA

Between 1913 and 1938 Morris led expeditions to New Mexico and Arizona for the University of Colorado. He became a friend and colleague of Alfred V. Kidder, the most distinguished American archaeologist of the first half of the 20th century. In March 1927 Kidder wrote to invite Morris to the first Pecos Conference, organized by Kidder to attempt to bring some order to the burgeoning body of Southwestern data:

> *This is a little premature, but I want to get a bid for your time in as early as possible. Roberta and Judd and I are planning to have a get-together of as many field workers in Southwestern archaeology as possible at Pecos for two or three days, beginning August 29th, in order to thrash out at leisure the various questions of problems, method, and nomenclature which we discussed in a preliminary way in Judd's office this autumn. I hope very much that you can arrange your affairs in such a way as to be there, as the whole project could hardly be a success in your absence.*

These annual conferences, although infrequently celebrated at Pecos, have become a fixture in Southwestern archaeology.

KAWAIKA-A

In the fall of 1928 Morris excavated at the site of Kawaika-a on Hopi Reservation land. His work there has been summarized by Hannah Huse, and the following is taken from her work. Excavating at Kawaika-a fulfilled two objectives for Morris: to excavate a site near the Hopi Second Mesa, and to search for post-Basket Maker remains. He excavated both in eight refuse deposits and mounds in and adjacent to the site and also excavated in room blocks (22 rooms and one kiva) to obtain timber specimens for A. E. Douglas's tree-ring dating program. The main occupation at Kawaika-a was dated from A.D. 1284 to A.D. 1495.

Excavation in some of the refuse areas produced 63 human burials, accompanied by pottery and other personal goods. "Many perishable objects," Morris noted, "had been placed with the dead. Matting, both sewn and plaited; fur or feather string blankets; and both coiled and wicker basketry could now and then be distinguished among the mould. Ear corn had been an almost unvarying accompaniment, sometimes in considerable quantity."

Of the ceramics recovered, Huse selected 115 Jeddito Polychrome vessels for her research. She found a definite relationship between the production of individual potters and the places in the archaeological site where they were found. She analyzed the shapes of the vessels, as well as the painted decorations on the insides and outsides of the pots. Al Qöyawayma, a well-known contemporary Hopi potter, looked at the Jeddito Polychrome vessels with members of the University of Colorado Museum's Anthropology staff in the fall of 1984. He made interesting comments regarding the generally high quality of the production of the *ceramic vessels themselves* but the relatively low quality *of design* on most of them. How this correlates with Hannah Huse's research on prehistoric potters remains to be seen, but it points out the continued research value of the data Morris generated.

ANASAZI AND BASKET MAKERS

After 1929 the Division of Historical Research of the Carnegie Institution of Washington decided to expand its activities into the Pueblo area of the Southwest, and Morris played a major role. Research efforts focused on elaborating the Anasazi-Pueblo sequence and the intensive study of Basket Maker sites near Durango and in the La Plata district, both in Colorado.

In 1931 Earl Morris excavated a series of caves in the Red Rock Valley on the Navajo Reservation in northeastern Arizona, seeking evidence of the elusive Basket Maker people. He found the perishable remains he was looking for—sandals, baskets, and textile fragments. He also found fragile mud vessels which had been molded inside baskets and which may have been a link in the original development of true fired pottery. Morris was particularly interested in this transitional phase of Anasazi life between Basket Maker II and Basket Maker III, which, as he says, "... bridged the only remaining gap in the cultural history of the ancient peoples of the San Juan region." Years later his daughter Elizabeth Ann Morris wrote her doctoral dissertation at the University of Arizona on the Basket Maker III people who had lived in the San Juan area and whose sandals, baskets, mud pots, and other possessions were collected by Earl.

Until the summer of 1939 the Basket Maker people had been seen as unsettled nomads with no permanent dwellings; no evidence of grinding corn had been found. That year the excavation of three sites in the Durango area greatly changed archaeologists' ideas about Basket Maker society: two rock shelters overlooking Hidden Valley some six miles north of Durango, and Talus Village, cut into the steep hillside that borders the Animas Valley on the west.

The prehistoric inhabitants had an inexhaustable supply of timber for fuel and construction. Yucca plants and tule rushes from scattered ponds provided ample material for the characteristic coarse weaving of the Basket Makers. Game was plentiful. Agriculture, while not as important as it would become, could flourish in the alluvial valley bottoms well-watered by nearly 20 inches of rain annually. The growing season of about 116 days, although short, was adequate for the kinds of corn and squash the Indians raised.

Morris's careful dissection of the superimposed structures at the three sites, a remarkable achievement in itself, revealed village and house plans of the Basket Makers for the first time. In rockshelters and Talus Village alike, the Basket Makers began by making a terrace to put the house on by first digging a semicircle into the slope of the hillside or cave floor. Dirt from this cut was piled in front of the excavated area. A level space for the intended house was prepared, partly on natural earth and partly on fill. Stones placed around the rim of the terrace held the fill in place, and an oval trench or groove was dug to enclose the area. Short sections of logs were plastered into these grooves to form the wall foundation and were followed by smaller logs and branches laid in mud to resemble masonry. Ends of the logs overlapped the ends of those below. They were cribbed—that is, each log was laid across the slight angle formed by the two underlying logs. As the wall rose it was pulled inward so that the finished house was a dome surfaced with clay.

The floor was formed into a saucer shape, rising toward the walls and plastered. Near the center was a basin filled with sand where, in winter or at night, stones heated in an outside fire were buried and continued to radiate gentle heat for hours. One or more storage pits might be built inside the house. Some were large, deep, jug-shaped pits, small at the mouth but up to five or six feet in diameter near the bottom. Others were simple pits left plain, plastered, or lined with stone slabs plastered in place. They were sometimes covered by a beehive-shaped clay dome. Corn, pumpkins, and wild vegetables were stored in these cists, as well as tools and weapons. An abandoned storage pit was often used as a grave, perhaps when the frozen ground outside made digging difficult.

Mats, blankets of rabbit fur or feathers twisted around cords of yucca fibers, skins, baskets, and utensils of gourd rind or wood found in the dry parts of rock shelters suggest the nature of the Basket Makers' perishable furnishings. Grinding stones were sometimes built into pedestals of clay to raise them to the proper angle for grinding.

The houses were highly flammable and often burned, causing preservation through charring and baking of many details that would otherwise be lost to the archaeologist. Charred house timbers provided tree-ring dates, the earliest for the three sites excavated by Morris being A.D. 46 and the latest about A.D. 330. The A.D. 46 date was the earliest for Southwestern Colorado at the time and pushed the known occupation of Basket Maker sites back almost two centuries.

Morris's 1939 work disproved previous notions about the Basket Maker peoples, showing that they built permanent homes and knew how to grind corn. The research also showed over 700 years of cultural stability for the Basket Maker peoples.

LATER LIFE

In contrast to his childhood digging, Morris developed a master's touch at excavation and a keen appreciation for its sensitive requirements:

> *Pick and shovel are the tools of a lowly and misunderstood profession. Casually it would seem that any lump of animate matter with sufficient intelligence to guide food and drink to its lips could wield them with all the effectiveness lying within the possibilities of such gross implements. Never was a notion more erroneous. There are almost as many different kinds of picks and shovels as there are of artists' brushes, and each one is shaped for a definite and specific skill. Sufficient mental alertness quickly to recognize the object which his pick point or shovel blade has laid bare, an ability to evaluate the mechanical relationship between the components of the mass to be moved,*

19

and good coordination between eye and hand, are, far more than size or strength, the essentials to the making of a master craftsman in the art of digging ditch or driving tunnel. And if ever the touch of the master is needed, it is in archaeological excavation.

Being an archaeologist has been likened to being a detective, or, less romantically, to working on a jig-saw puzzle. Clues from broken fragments of pottery, stone, and other materials are fitted together to understand the lives of prehistoric people. This aspect of archaeology was highly evident in Morris's career and writings.

Morris was twice honored by the University of Colorado. In 1931 he was awarded the Norlin Medal, given annually to an alumnus who has achieved unusual distinction in a chosen field. In 1942 the honorary degree of Doctor of Science was conferred upon him by the regents in further recognition of his achievement.

In December 1953, at a meeting of the American Anthropological Association in Tucson, Arizona, Morris was presented with the first Alfred Vincent Kidder Award. It has since been awarded every three years to a scientist for excellence in the fields of Central American and Southwestern archaeology. Morris was cited as "... one of the very few scholars in the field of American archaeology who has contributed to both Southwestern and Meso-American Study."

Throughout his career Earl Morris studied the Anasazi peoples of the La Plata River Valley and surrounding areas in southern Colorado and northern New Mexico. Through the excavation of numerous sites and the study of innumerable prehistoric artifacts, Morris documented the lives and durable possessions of the Basket Maker and Pueblo people. Anasazi pottery was especially interesting to Morris, and he developed a chronological scheme for the various designs and vessel forms which he found.

Earl Morris's distinguished career ended with his sudden death from a heart attack on June 25, 1956, at his home in Boulder.

THE LEGACY
OF
EARL H. MORRIS

In 1961 the National Science Foundation gave an $8,500 grant to the University of Colorado to support publication of the Earl H. Morris Papers. In the following four years an additional $34,789 was awarded to the Earl H. Morris archives project. These grants enabled Roy Carlson and Joe Ben Wheat to publish some of the most important of Morris's unpublished data.

To further stimulate and recognize excellence in archaeology, the Morris family now supports the Earl H. Morris award, established in 1958 by Mrs. Lucille Morris. It is awarded to outstanding graduate students in the Department of Anthropology at the University of Colorado.

The information gathered by Morris continues to be consulted and used by researchers. Hannah Huse's work on the stylistic analysis of Kawaika-a ceramics has already been mentioned; further research on these same ceramics is planned as part of the Conservation Analytical Laboratory of the Smithsonian Institution's research project on protohistoric Hopi ceramics.

Thus, through the interest of his family, and through the heritage of his field collections and archival materials, Earl H. Morris continues to contribute to the contemporary era of archaeology. As the photographs show, the world has changed greatly since Morris first went into the field; that his data are still of interest is the highest tribute to his methods and talents as a scientist.

Joe Ben Wheat
Senior Curator of Anthropology
University of Colorado Museum

A section of the 1983 "Among Ancient Ruins" exhibition, University of Colorado Museum.

PORTFOLIO

Farmington, New Mexico, circa 1915, where Earl Morris grew up.

I was born in Chama, New Mexico, October 24, 1889. My parents were Scott N. Morris and Juliette Halstead Morris. Both were of old New York families. They came with the gold rush to Leadville in 1879 and for many years thereafter my father followed freighting and the construction of railroads, canals and highways. My boyhood was spent in mining, sawmill or construction camps, or in small towns near to my father's work throughout Colorado and the southwestern states. —Earl Morris, 1932

Ann and Earl Morris.

Ann Axtell—I first heard that name in an Indian Trading Post by the river San Juan in New Mexico. As I coaxed an old car homeward toward my bachelor's shack at the Aztec Ruin, an image of the owner of the name floated ever between my eyes and the sparkling splendor of the desert night. "The star you've watched for at last has risen," echoed over and over in my thoughts. Ten years have passed. The star still gleams and I have learned that it shines not in reflected light, but from a deep fire that burns within.
—Earl Morris, reflections, 1933

Earl Morris in the driver's seat of "Old Joe," on expedition in Canyon del Muerto, Arizona, 1924.

Getting Old Joe unstuck from a "wash," Canyon del Muerto, Arizona.

I am thoroughly convinced that the present car system is a failure.
—Earl Morris, letter to Nels C. Nelson, 1915

Getting around is more difficult than it used to be. In 1912 there were livery stables and though horses were slow you could get there. Today it is mostly car service and it seems, if the car is not busy, it is busted; and anyway it can't go where I want to go, often. —Nels C. Nelson, letter to Earl Morris, 1917

The notion seems rather current
that the archaeologist lives about
the most thrilling and carefree
existence to be found in modern
times. (But) those who live by
archaeology encounter more
difficulties and disappointments,
and fully as much hard work,
both physical and mental, as fall
to the lot of the average mortal.
—Earl Morris, 1931

Canyon del Muerto, Arizona, 1924. The latrine house was picked up—lock, stock and barrel—and was transported on the extended back of the trusty truck to its fresh new location, but not without some clowning around!

During the 1920s automobiles became regular parts of
archaeological expeditions.

Goat-skinning at Gobernador, New Mexico, 1915.

In the course of an existence which seldom has lain in the path of the usual, a wide variety of things has come to my hands for the doing.
—Earl Morris, 1931

Archaeologists' camp in Canyon del Muerto, Arizona, 1924. Artifacts excavated from Basket Maker sites were crated up for the slow trip to the laboratory.

Earl Morris and Navajo helpers.

Morris believed in hiring local people as much as possible and, thereby, supporting the local economy.

Farl Morris with Navajo assistant.

Archaeologists' camp at Canyon del Muerto, 1924.

All afternoon Fraser and Houser dug cactus from camp ground while Omer got his kitchen in order and the rest of us put up the other five tents. By six they were all done, beds up, and camp already in good shape. Omer had a fine supper—mashed spuds, fried mutton, corn bread and coffee. After supper I got a chance to shave for the first time since Aztec (four days earlier) and felt more like a human being. —Earl Morris, field journal, 1932

Morris with unidentified group of companions.

In 1921 I accompanied Charles L. Bernheimer (New York entrepreneur and patron of the American Museum of Natural History) on an exploring trip in northern Arizona. We traveled down Navajo Canyon, a tributary of the Colorado River which drains the country south of Navajo Mountain.
—Earl Morris, 1939

Rainbow Bridge, photographed on the 1921
Bernheimer Expedition.

This is to remind you to take a Kodak or other camera with you on your trip, provided of course that you have one. I strongly urge this, as there are many opportunities for taking interesting pictures. I, of course, shall take mine.
—Earl Morris, letter to C. L. Bernheimer, 1921

Navajo horses in Canyon de Chelly, Arizona, 1923/1924. One of the attractions of Southwestern archaeology has been the combination of exciting research and dramatic scenery.

Earl Morris and fellow archaeologist, A.V. "Ted" Kidder, at Awatovi, Arizona, 1938. Photograph courtesy of Don Woodard, Cortez, Colorado.

As to the quality of the friendship which has existed between us, I am in complete agreement. To me it has been a golden thread running untarnished and unstrained through the tangled skein of existence ever since the day of our first meeting, now so long ago. I am grateful to life for an experience so rich and rare. —Earl Morris, letter to A. V. Kidder, 1955

Ann and Earl were joined by a group of visiting archaeologists. Frank Roberts stands second from the left. In the more formal times of yesteryear, it was not uncommon for visitors to wear suits and ties to the field.

Eighteenth century towers in the Gobernador district, Rio Grande Valley, New Mexico, 1915.

The ruins in Canyon Gobernador proved to be considerable of a surprise. They are post-Spanish, as is evidenced by numerous metal objects, and the pottery is greatly mixed. From one spot came European porcelain, several types of red and yellow vessels, glazed ware, and what at present appears to be biscuit ware. In addition to the recent, there are a great many pre-Pueblo remains.
—Earl Morris, letter to Nels C. Nelson, 1915

Hill-top look-out site in the Gobernador region. The defensive locations of such sites reflect the seriousness of the conflict with the Spanish in the late 17th century.

Looking northeast across La Plata Valley from Site 41.

The La Plata district lies in the heart of a wide sweep of country wherein an aboriginal people, never curbed by conquest and little swayed by outside influences, between the beginning of the Christian era and the year 1300, rose from seminomadism to a creditable degree of civilization along the lines dictated by the response of their particular cast of mentality to the possibilities the material environment affected. —Earl Morris, letter, 1939

Site 41 in the La Plata Valley, New Mexico, 1930.

. . . one more element of the mosaic picture of the life and customs of the prehistoric Pueblo people which it is our aim and effort to reconstruct in its most intimate detail.
—Earl Morris, letter to Clark Wissler, 1922

Front of Building 1, Site 39, La Plata. Kiva 2 is in the foreground.

Room 8, Building I, Site 41, La Plata District. Cache/storage pots in corner, with stone lids. 1930.

Kiva 14, Building XVI, Site 41, La Plata District. Alignment
of sipapu, firepit, deflector, and ventilator tunnel.

The pueblo at Aztec, New Mexico.

The importance of the exploration of the Aztec Ruin is three-fold: first because of the scientific data which it yields; second, because of the pleasing and and instructive exhibits which it furnishes for the halls of the Museum; and third, because for the world at large it is providing in situ a permanent and attractive monument to the arts and material accomplishments of the aborigines of the Southwest, which will prove as the years pass, to be of constantly increasing educational value. —Earl Morris, letter to Clark Wissler, 1918

A formal milling room with a row of metate bins. Women were able to kneel side by side here and grind their corn with stone tools. Aztec Ruin, New Mexico.

Reconstruction of the Great Kiva at Aztec, New Mexico. Earl Morris documented what the original structure had looked like and directed its stabilization. The actual reconstruction of the roof occurred at a later date.

Earl Morris with work crew at Aztec.

Our crew of workmen is the best that I have ever had under my direction. They are the result of a strenuous process of selection, and being already familiar with the work, have a much higher individual efficiency than could be expected of a "green" crew. —Earl Morris, report to Clark Wissler, 1919

Broken Flute cave, northeastern Arizona.

The outstanding problem now is to determine whether the Pottery Makers were directly descended from the Basket Makers who preceded them. The data to settle this point can be had only from cliff shelters where perishable materials such as baskets and textiles remain intact. I anticipate that somewhere in the recesses of the canyons there are sites where typical Basket Maker products will be found in association with the earliest types of pottery, this condition being representative of the transition between the two cultures.
—Earl Morris, letter to Clark Wissler, 1922

Sifting carefully for small objects during excavations at Aztec helped to recover small bones, beads, and broken pottery.

When searching for very small objects, a screen mounted horizontally, over which one rakes the earth back and forth with a trowel, has seemed to me to work best. For larger objects, say where a quarter inch mesh is used, more speed is attained by placing it at an incline with one person trowelling and watching the material that does not pass through.

I have always thought that if I faced a really extensive job of screening, I would build a mechanical sifter—something run with a small engine that would agitate a series of screens, one above the other, so that each could be slipped out and the contents examined at the desired interval. I have never made a model of such a device, but I think any good machinist could set up such a machine without great cost. And I believe that it would more than pay for itself on the job. —Earl Morris, letter to Nels Nelson, 1941

Most pottery vessels are broken when found in archaeological sites. Earl Morris loved to restore the fragments, and the collections in the University of Colorado Museum show the care he devoted to this part of his research.

Earl Morris recognized that in the process of studying an archaeological site, it was gradually destroyed. A photographic record was an important part of the information obtained. His field photographs are a reminder of his skill.

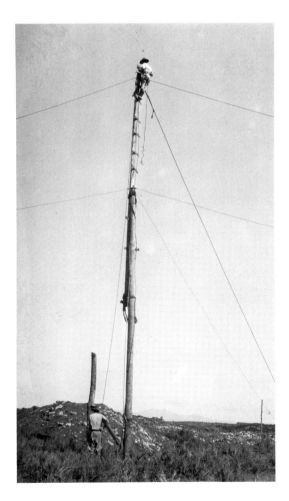

I nailed more steps to the tree and got to a height of 60 feet, which gives a good vantage point for the picture. Too windy to try it today because the tree top swayed constantly.
—Earl Morris, field journal

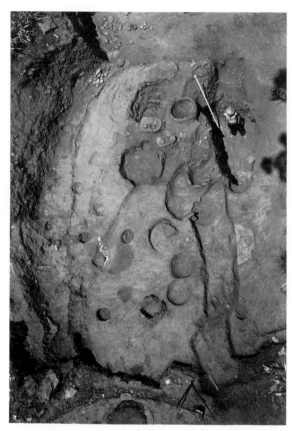

The high aerial views provided excellent summaries of site organization. Note grinding stones, hearths, and storage pits. Durango.

Wrapping portions of house beams for later shipment to the Tree-Ring Laboratory at the University of Arizona, 1921.

Although I served only as a gatherer of material, I feel that what I did toward making the building of the tree-ring chronology possible constitutes my most important contribution to Southwestern archaeology.
—Earl Morris, letter to Emil Haury, 1956

Archaeologists often need to improvise equipment for the field work. Morris often used a bellows to gently remove the last film of dust from an excavated area.

Carefully exposed ceramic vessels, La Plata district.

Sufficient mental alertness quickly to recognize the object which his pick point or shovel blade has laid bare, an ability to evaluate the mechanical relationship between the components of the mass to be moved, and good coordination between eye and hand are, far more than size or strength, the essentials to the making of a master craftsman in the art of digging ditch or driving tunnel. —Earl Morris, 1931

Antelope House, Canyon de Chelly, 1931. Antelope House was named for a series of petroglyphs which stretch across the cliff wall behind the buildings. Four antelope, each measuring about seven feet in length, leap across the sandstone wall. In 1929 Ann Axtell Morris recorded and made reproductions of these famous painted creatures.

Cliff dwellings, Canyon del Muerto.

There is nowhere else an opportunity of so thoroughly exemplifying early conditions culturally and of displaying in a restricted locality a very long cycle of the gradual ascent of a primitive people toward civilization. These canyons have been a nucleus not only of the old Pueblo domain but more recently of the Navajo. They were occupied I believe continuously from the time that man first appears in the Southwest, barring possibly the Folsom Quarry-Gypsum Cave horizon, that is, from Basket Maker II to the close of Pueblo III. The late masonry Cliff House phase is amply exemplfied elsewhere, notably in the Mesa Verde National Park. In contrast the Canyon de Chelly (and del Muerto) is particularly rich in remains that date from the beginning rather than the end of the culture cycle.
—Earl Morris, in defense of establishing Canyons de Chelly and del Muerto as National Monuments, 1935

Ann Axtell Morris began copying and recording rock art in Canyon del Muerto in 1929 for the American Museum of Natural History. Earlier, Mrs. Morris was commissioned to draw and reproduce the designs from fragile Maya wall paintings while on expedition in the Yucatan with her husband.

Excavation of a structure in a cave, Canyon del Muerto.

Two more days on the rock pile. The whole crew of us are sure miserable and tired. A terrific rain and hail this afternoon which whipped back to the rear wall of the cave.
—Earl Morris, field journal, 1938

A kiva in Canyon del Muerto. Morris was able to compare contemporary buildings used by Hopi and other Pueblo Indians in order to identify important features in such prehistoric structure—the altar, a ventilator shaft, the air deflector, and subterranean footdrums.

Dust has always been a problem in cave excavations. Modern archaeologists use breathing devices, while in Morris's time handerkerchiefs and even hoods (such as worn by the person in the center), had to suffice.

White House ruin, Canyon de Chelly, Arizona.

In the field conditions are never quite the same twice in succession, no set of conditions is identical with any that has been met before, or will in future be encountered. There is no written book, no set of tables, no slide-rule, to point the answer to one's problems.
—Earl Morris, 1931

Reconstruction of the tower, Mummy Cave, Canyon del Muerto, Arizona (1932).

Mummy Cave was probably the most favored shelter in that whole canyon system, and I doubt if it was ever really unoccupied from the time the Basket Makers first came in until the close of Pueblo III. There was constant rebuilding and readjustment of the structures.
—Earl Morris, letter to A.E. Douglas, 1935

"Tomb of the Weaver" as it appeared from the surface. The tomb contained a large quantity of baskets, mats, and other perishable goods.

"Tomb of the Weaver." Definition of cover of the tomb after the upper layer of matting was removed.

"Tomb of the Weaver." Roof of the tomb with part of next layer removed. Covering was carefully constructed of alternating layers.

"Tomb of the Weaver." Removal of the remaining layers of branches revealed the four main support beams.

"Tomb of the Weaver." Inside the tomb we can see weaving tools and products, as well as large fragments of pottery being used to cover baskets. We see how important it is, in this series of photographs, to recover different materials in their original relationships. It is also important to see that broken pieces of pottery continued to be used.

"Tomb of the Weaver." With the ceramic covers removed, we see the baskets with some of their original seed contents still present.

Stratigraphy—Wherever there are deposits of any nature, the accumulation of which has covered an appreciable interval, the oldest, of necessity, must be at the bottom, and the most recent at the top. In this way positive age cannot be established, but the relative age can be fixed with full certainty. Hence the field man in archaeology burrows beneath surface remains to find what lies between the visible and the bed rock. —Earl Morris, 1931

Room excavation at Kawaika-a.

Pottery vessels from the Kawaika-a excavations (all now in the collections of the University of Colorado Museum).
The running board of the field vehicle doubled as Morris's photographic stand.

Detail of an elegant hand motif on one of the pottery vessels from Kawaika-a.

Two dippers, or ladles, from the excavations at Kawaika-a.

Pottery collected by Earl Morris and displayed in the first University of Colorado Museum building, Hale Science Building, prior to 1937.

Raising a carved stela at the site of Quirigua, Guatemala.
The carved glyphs on the monument recorded historical,
calendrical, and political information.

Close-up of one of the elaborate monuments at Quirigua, Guatemala.

Reconstruction in progress, Temple of the Warriors,
Chichen Itza, Yucatan.

PUBLICATIONS BY AND ABOUT EARL H. MORRIS

ABOUT EARL MORRIS

Lister, Florence C., and Robert H. Lister. 1968. *Earl Morris & Southwestern Archaeology*. University of New Mexico Press. Albuquerque.

Morris, Ann Axtell. 1934. *Digging in the Southwest*. Doubleday, Duran, & Company. New York.

———. 1931. *Digging in Yucatan*. Junior Literary Guild. New York.

Rodeck, Hugo G. 1956. Earl Morris and the University of Colorado Museum, An Appreciation. *Southwestern Lore*, 22:3.

University of Colorado Museum. 1983. *The Morris Code*.

BASED ON THE WORK OF EARL MORRIS

Carlson, Roy L. 1963. *Basket Maker III Sites Near Durango, Colorado*. University of Colorado Studies, Series in Anthropology No. 8, The Earl Morris Papers No. 1.

———. 1965. *Eighteenth Century Navajo Fortresses of the Gobernador District*. University of Colorado Studies, Series in Anthropology No. 10, The Earl Morris Papers No. 2.

Huse, Hannah. 1976. *Identification of the Individual in Archaeology: A Case-Study from the Prehistoric Hopi Site of Kawaika-a*. Ph.D. dissertation, University of Colorado.

Morris, Elizabeth Ann. 1959. *Basketmaker Caves in the Prayer Rock District, Northwestern New Mexico*. Ph.D. dissertation, University of Arizona.

———. A Pueblo I Site near Bennett's Peak, Northwestern New Mexico. *El Palacio*, 66:5.

FURTHER READING ON COLORADO AND SOUTHWESTERN ARCHAEOLOGY

Cassells, E. Steve. 1983. *The Archaeology of Colorado*. Johnson Books. Boulder.

Cordell, Linda S. 1984. *Prehistory of the Southwest*. Academic Press. New York.

Lister, Robert H. and Florence C. 1983. *Those Who Came Before*. University of Arizona Press, Tucson.

Noble, David Grant, ed. 1984. *New Light on Chaco Canyon*. School of American Research Press. Santa Fe.

Smith, Jack E., ed. 1983. *Proceedings of the Anasazi Symposium—1981*. Mesa Verde Museum Association, Inc. Mesa Verde National Park.

WORKS BY EARL H. MORRIS

1911   The Cliff Dwellers of the San Juan. *Colorado.* 2:7:27-30. Denver, Colorado.

1915   The Excavation of a Small Ruin near Aztec, San Juan County, New Mexico. *American Anthropologist*, n.s. 17:4:66-84. Lancaster, Pa.

1916   Explorations in New Mexico—Field Work in the La Plata Valley done by the American Museum-University of Colorado Expedition. 1916. Tribune Print. Farmington, New Mexico.

1917   The Place of Coiled Ware in Southwestern Pottery. *American Anthropologist*, n.s. 19:1:24-29. Lancaster, Pa.

1917a The Ruins at Aztec. *El Palacio*, 4:3:43-69. Santa Fe, N.M.

1917b Discoveries at the Aztec Ruin. *American Museum Journal*, 17:3:169-80. New York, N.Y.

1917c Explorations in New Mexico. *American Museum Journal*, 17:7:461-71. New York, N.Y.

1918   Further Discoveries at the Aztec Ruin. *American Museum Journal*, 18:7:602-10. New York, N.Y.

1919   Preliminary Account of the Antiquities of the Region between the Mancos and La Plata Rivers in Southwestern Colorado. *Thirty-Third Annual Report*, Bureau of American Ethnology, pp. 155-206. Washington, D.C.

1919a The Aztec Ruin. *Anthropological Papers*, American Museum of Natural History, 26:pt. 1. New York, N.Y.

1919b Further Discoveries at the Aztec Ruin. *El Palacio*, 6:17-23, 26. Santa Fe, New Mexico.

1921   Chronology of the San Juan Area. *Proceedings of the National Academy of Sciences*, 7:18-22.

1921a The House of the Great Kiva at the Aztec Ruin. *Anthropological Papers*, 26: pt. 2. American Museum of Natural History. New York, N.Y.

1922   An Unexplored Area of the Southwest. *American Museum Journal*, 22:498-515. New York, N.Y.

1924   Burials in the Aztec Ruin: the Aztec Ruin Annex. *Anthropological Papers*, 26: pts. 3 & 4. American Museum of Natural History, New York, N.Y.

1924a Report of E. H. Morris on the Excavations at Chichen Itza, Mexico. *Carnegie Institution of Washington Yearbook*, No. 23:211-213. Washington, D.C.

1925 Exploring in the Canyon of Death. *National Geographic Magazine*, 48:263-300. Washington, D.C.

1925a Report of E. H. Morris on the Temple of the Warriors (station 4.) *Carnegie Institution of Washington Yearbook*, No. 24:252-59. Washington, D.C.

1925b Report of E. H. Morris on the mural paintings of the Temple of the Warriors (station 4). *Carnegie Institution of Washington Yearbook*, No. 24:260-62. Washington, D.C.

1925c Report of E. H. Morris on the temple on the northeast bank of the Xtoloc cenote (station 3). *Carnegie Institution of Washington Yearbook*, No. 24:263-65. Washington, D.C.

1926 Report of E. H. Morris on the Excavation of the Temple of the Warriors and the northwest colonade, (Stations 4 and 10). *Carnegie Institution of Washington Yearbook*, No. 25:282-86. Washington, D.C.

1927 Report of E. H. Morris on the Temple of the Warriors and the northwest colonade, (Stations 4 and 10). Carnegie Institution of Washington Yearbook, No. 26:240-46. Washington, D.C.

1927a The Beginnings of Pottery Making in the San Juan Area, Unfired Prototypes and the Wares of the Earliest Ceramic Period. *Anthropological Papers*, 28: pt. 2. American Museum of Natural History, New York, N.Y.

1928 Turquoise Plaque. *El Palacio*, 24:349-50. Santa Fe, N.M.

1928a Temple of Warriors Rebuilt. *El Palacio*, 25:425-26. Santa Fe, N.M.

1928b Report of E. H. Morris on the excavation and repair of the Temple of the Warriors (station 4). *Carnegie Institution of Washington Yearbook*, No. 27:293-97. Washington, D.C.

1928c Notes on Excavations in the Aztec Ruin. *Anthropological Papers*, 26: pt. 5. American Museum of Natural History, New York, N.Y.

1928d An Aboriginal Salt Mine at Camp Verde, Arizona. *Anthropological Papers*, 30: pt. 3. American Museum of Natural History, New York, N.Y.

1929 Archaeological field work in North America during 1928: Arizona. *American Anthropologist*, n.s. 31:339-40. Menasha, Wisconsin.

1929a Early Pueblos. *El Palacio*, 27:279-81. Santa Fe, N.M.

1931   Archaeological Research in southwestern United States: the San Juan Basin. *Carnegie Institution of Washington Yearbook*, No. 30:139-41. Washington, D.C.

1931a   The Temple of the Warriors. *Art and Archaeology*, 31:298-305. Washington, D.C.

1931b   El Templo de los Guerreros. (In Los Mayas de la region central de America). *Carnegie Institution of Washington, Supplementary Publications*, No. 4:7-12. Washington, D.C.

1931c   *The Temple of the Warriors.* Charles Scribner's Sons. New York, N.Y.

1931d   *The Temple of the Warriors.* Part 2 in The Maya of Middle America. Carnegie Institution of Washington News Service Bulletin, School Edition. 2:17-21. Washington, D.C.

1931e   Earl H. Morris, Jean Charlot, and A. A. Morris. *The Temple of the Warriors*, 2 vols. Carnegie Institution of Washington Pub. 406. Washington, D.C.

1934   E. H. Morris and G. Stromsvik. Quirigua. Annual Report of the Division of Historical Research—Section Aboriginal American History. *Yearbook*, No. 33:86-89. Carnegie Institution of Washington, Washington, D.C.

1934a   Speaker Chief's House, *Mesa Verde Notes*, 5:1:4-6. Mesa Verde National Park, Colorado.

1935   *Adventure.* The Eleusis of Chi Omega. 37:4. George Banta Publishing Co. Menasha, Wisconsin.

1936   Archaeological Background of Dates in Early Arizona Chronology. *Tree-Ring Bulletin.* 2:4:346. Tucson, Arizona.

1937   Southwestern Research. Annual Report of the Division of Historical Research. *Yearbook* No. 36:17-18. Carnegie Institution of Washington, Washington, D.C.

1938   Mummy Cave. *Natural History*, 42:127-38. New York, N.Y.

1939   Archaeological Studies in the La Plata District. *Carnegie Institution of Washington*, Publication 519. Washington, D.C.

1940   Southwestern Archaeology. Annual Report of the Chairman of the Division of Historical Research. *Yearbook* No. 39:274-75. Carnegie Institution of Washington, Washington, D.C.

1941   Southwestern Archaeology. Annual Report of the Chairman of the Division of Historical Research. *Yearbook* No. 40:304-5. Carnegie Institution of Washington, Washington, D.C.

1941a   Prayer Sticks in Walls of Mummy Cave Tower, Canyon del Muerto. *American Antiquity*, 6:3:227-30. Menasha, Wisc.

1941b   Earl H. Morris and R. F. Burgh. Anasazi Basketry-Basket Maker II through Pueblo III. Carnegie Institution of Washington Pub. 533. Washington, D.C.

1941c   Book Review of Archaeological Work in the Ackmen-Lowry Area, Southwestern Colorado and of Modified Basket Maker Sites, Ackmen-Lowry Area, Southwestern Colorado. Paul S. Martin, Anthropological Series, Field Museum of Natural History, 23:2 & 3. Chicago, Ill. In *American Antiquity*, 6:4:378-382. Menasha, Wisc.

1942   Book Review of Excavations in the Forestdale Valley, East-Central Arizona. Emil W. Haury, University of Arizona Bulletin, No. 4, 1940. In *American Anthropologist*, 44:3:485-87. Menasha, Wisc.

1924a   Southwestern United States. Annual Report of the Chairman of the Division of Historical Research. *Yearbook* No. 41:272-3. Carnegie Institution of Washington, Washington, D.C.

1943   Southwestern Archaeology. Annual Report of the Chairman of the Division of Historical Research. *Yearbook* No. 42:179-80. Carnegie Institution of Washington, Washington, D.C.

1944   Southwestern Archaeology. Annual Report of the Chairman of the Division of Historical Research. *Yearbook* NO. 43:174-6. Carnegie Institution of Washington, Washington, D.C.

1944a   Anasazi Sandals. Clearing House for Western Museums. *News Letters* 68/69; 239-41. Denver, Colorado.

1944b   Adobe Bricks in a Pre-Spanish Wall Near Aztec, New Mexico. *American Antiquity*, 9:4:434-438. Menasha.

1946   Early Cultures of Southwestern United States. Annual Report of the Chairmen of the Division of Historical Research. *Yearbook* 45:214-15. Carnegie Institution of Washington, Washington, D.C.

1947   Early Cultures of Southwestern United States. Annual Report of the Chairman of the Division of Historical Research. *Yearbook* No. 46:192-3. Carnegie Institution of Washington, Washington, D.C.

1948   Early Cultures of Southwestern United States. Annual Report of the Chairman of the Division of Historical Research. *Yearbook* No. 47:220-21. Carnegie Institution of Washington, Washington, D.C.

1948a   Tomb of the Weaver. *Natural History*, 57:2:66-71. New York, N.Y.

1948b   Book Review of Prehistoric Indians of the Southwest. Marie Wormington, Colorado Museum of Natural History, Pop. Series, No. 7, 1947. In *Southwestern Lore* 8:4:70. Colorado Archaeological Society. Gunnison, Colorado.

1949   Basket Maker II Dwellings near Durango, Colorado. *Tree-Ring Bulletin*, 15:4:33-34. Tucson, Arizona.

1950   Journey to Copan. (in *Morleyana*, pp. 154-9) American School of Prehistoric Research and the Museum of New Mexico, Santa Fe, N.M.

1950a   Southwestern Prehistory. Annual Report of the Chairman of the Division of Historical Research, *Yearbook* No. 49:205-6. Carnegie Institution of Washington, Washington, D.C.

1951   Basket Maker III Human Figurines from Northeastern Arizona. *American Antiquity*, 17:1:33-40. Menasha, Wisc.

1951a   Book Review of Excavations in Mesa Verde National Park. Deric O'Bryan. In *American Antiquity*, 17:1:72-3. Menasha, Wisc.

1952   Note on the Durango Dates. *Tree-Ring Bulletin*, 18:4:36. Tucson, Arizona.

1952a   Southwestern Prehistory. Annual Report of the Director of the Department of Archaeology. *Yearbook* 51:272. Carnegie Institution of Washington, Washington, D.C.

1953   Utilized Fiber Materials, in Wendorf, Fred, Archaeological Studies in the Petrified Forest National Monument, p. 154. Museum of Northern Arizona, *Bulletin* No. 27. Flagstaff, Arizona.

1953a   Artifacts of Perishable Material from Te'ewi. Archaeological Institute of America. School of American Research, Monographs, 17:103. Santa Fe, N.M.

1954   Earl H. Morris and Robert F. Burgh. Basketmaker II Sites Near Durango, Colorado. Carnegie Institution of Washington Publication 604. Washington, D.C.

1955   Southwestern Prehistory. Annual Report of the Director of the Department of Archaeology. *Yearbook* 54:295-97. Carnegie Institution of Washington, Washington, D.C.

PARTICIPANTS IN EARL MORRIS EXHIBITION

In 1983 the University of Colorado Museum mounted an exhibition entitled "Among Ancient Ruins," supported by a grant from the Colorado Humanities Program. The effort that went into producing this exhibit has made the present publication possible.

Dr. Ann Lane Hedlund, now curator of the Millicent Rogers Museum in Taos, New Mexico, curated the original exhibition. David Mayo and Janet Garber-Taffet of the University of Colorado Museum mounted the exhibition. Dick Carter and his staff at MCDB on the Boulder campus contributed significant photographic expertise to the original exhibition. Diana Leonard organized much of photo archive data for the original exhibit.

ACKNOWLEDGEMENTS

The efforts of Ann Lane, David Mayo, and Janet Garber-Taffet in organizing the museum's "Among Ancient Ruins" exhibit and the support of the Colorado Humanities Council resulted in the striking three-dimensional exhibition that was the impetus for converting the two-dimensional aspects into published form.

Billy Moore helped peruse the Morris photograph collection for additional material to be used in this book, and Holley Lange made many valuable suggestions concerning the text and organization of the photographs. Richard Carter and Larry Howard of the University of Colorado did excellent work on the photographs for both the exhibition and this publication. The biography of Morris by Bob and Florence Lister, as well as *The Morris Code* prepared in conjunction with the exhibition, were important background documents for the publication.

We also would like to thank the staff of Johnson Books for their enthusiasm for this project.